D1827255

JOB EVALUATION MADE EASY FOR SMALL BUSINESS

Based on The Temple System Guide Chart Job Evaluation Method

(The Method)

By Ray Temple

rltemple51@gmail.com

In the 1970s Philip M. Oliver developed a compensation management system for the federal government. It became known as The Oliver System. At that same time he formed Philip M. Oliver and Associates to market and install the System. Ray Temple joined him as his senior associate. In 1998, Ray took over the management of the System with Phil's retirement, re-naming it The Temple System Guide Chart Job Evaluation Method (The Method). There are similar systems being offered by other consulting firms, but the "original" Oliver System is only available from Ray Temple.

TABLE OF CONTENTS

**WE CAN DO THE WORK FOR YOU THROUGH
JOB EVALUATION MADE EASY….**

THE HISTORY OF JOB EVALUATION

It might be helpful to review the background of Job Evaluation before proceeding with a detailed discussion of The Method. The basic concept of evaluation and ranking dates as far back as the recorded existence of social structures. Throughout the world, formal systems existed and were passed down from generation to generation. Two classic structures that survived the centuries are found in religious and military organizations.

Jobs were and are arranged to make it easier to organize, administer and reward (or pay) for work performed. The arrangement usually took the form of an evaluation based on the inter-relationships of work performed by various members of the social structure. The factors governing the interrelationships vary with the social structure and its leaders. In modern times, the process has become fairly well institutionalized in both the private and public sectors.

Since the early 1900s there have been four classic methodologies: Whole Job Ranking, Point Rating, Factor Comparison, and Job Classification. There are many standardized texts which describe these, so no attempt will be made here to duplicate this material. The Method can be expected to replace some of the other methods now in general usage. It has a high degree of validity and reliability, and is both easy to learn and cost effective to administer.

One major purpose for evaluating jobs is to provide a systematic array which can be used for establishing rates of pay accepted as equitable by employees. The degree of sophistication in the process of evaluation is directly related to the given organization's size. Companies start with Whole Job Ranking and move to more refined methods as the organization grows because it becomes increasingly more difficult to carry out the Whole Job Ranking process in a larger organization. Job evaluation, thus, is not an end in itself but an intermediate step to organization structuring and pay setting.

Several additional administrative reasons for evaluation can be cited. Managerial favoritism is made more difficult with a formal evaluation system. Discussions about jobs with employee representatives can be more readily approached, and facilitated, on a more pragmatic basis. Legal requirements concerning Fair Labor Standards practices, Equal Employment opportunities, and safety and health problems can be addressed in a forthright manner through an evaluation system.

Some Basic Evaluation Concepts

From both a philosophical and practical viewpoint, there are some basic concepts around which an evaluation system should be built.

1. Jobs relate with similar jobs, therefore they remain in relative juxtaposition, regardless of geographic location, if there are no changes in responsibility or difficulty. Pay-wise, their relationship may change because of supply and demand, but this is not usually permanent.

2. Dissimilar jobs, when commingled for evaluation purposes, destroy internal and external comparisons and alignments. For example, comparing a professional with office support position. Hence, the evaluation structure loses credibility.

3. There is a practical limit to the numbers of differing levels of effort which can be readily identified within job families. It is hard to visualize more than two levels of building custodian, for example.

4. All too frequently, there is poor correlation between specified recruitment requirements and actual duties assigned to jobs. Jobs are made up of duties which are composed of tasks. Recruitment should be geared to the knowledge and skill required to complete tasks. From an evaluation system viewpoint, it should be possible to measure fairly directly what is required for performance of duties at a given level. Then, the recruitment requirements are a byproduct. As a case in point, a building custodian should be able to read directions for using cleaning chemicals, but should not be required to know how to write, unless his job has tasks which specifically call for this skill. Hence, for both evaluation and recruitment purposes, high school graduation for many jobs may be questionable as a job requirement.

5. Describing jobs requires observing a few ground rules. Related tasks should be grouped into essential functions, i.e., duties. Essential functions should be listed in descending order of importance. It is not necessary, from an evaluation viewpoint, to list every essential function, but only those that will have an impact on the eventual results.

6. Finally, internal alignment is of greater importance than external alignment. That is, it is more important to correctly evaluate jobs internally within the organization, in as accurate a hierarchy as possible, than to arrange them in an order that portrays external (.i.e., other employers') hierarchies. For example, using job titles only, one organization may equate an executive secretary with a

senior accountant whereas in another organization the accountant level may be lower. The important point is to have consensus on one's own internal arrangement of jobs. Any problems arising from trying to establish competitive pay rates for jobs can be resolved on an individual basis, and this is discussed later. Evaluation should never be used to resolve pay problems. This could destroy the integrity of a system/method very quickly.

The Relationship of Pay to Evaluation

Since evaluation is not an end in itself, but a means to arrive at pay, it is important to look very briefly at a few pay principles.

1. Pay should be resolved after the evaluation process. Whenever it is apparent that the labor market indicates a pay rate for a job which is at variance with its evaluation process in the structure, the evaluation must stand. The pay problem can be resolved by removing the job from the structure on an exception basis or any similar technique which identifies the problem as an exception to the rule.

2. There should be a clear distinction between technical and administrative supervision. In the former, subordinates should be paid less than their supervisors. In the latter, it may be that a specialist will be paid more than his administrative supervisor. This is normal and appropriate. A President is paid more than the Chairman of the Board and a Chief Psychologist may be paid more than the Hospital Director. Where the supervisor cannot provide technical guidance or resolve technical problems, there is no

requirement for him/her to be paid more than a specialist who administratively reports to him/her.

3. One cannot relate pay to job titles – only to job evaluations. Therefore, either internally or externally, comparisons must be based on the evaluations themselves. A secretary in one department may be a different skill level (or grade) than one in another department. Likewise, a secretary in one company cannot be compared externally to a secretary in another organization on the basis of title alone.

4. Finally, pay for varying jobs in varying Job Categories does not necessarily relate in any meaningful way. Labor, Trade and Craft jobs command pay in the local labor market and move in a different orbit than Professional jobs. Thus all jobs cannot be evaluated accurately from the same set of Factor definitions and Guide Charts and then paid from the same pay structure. As will be demonstrated in the next Part, jobs can only be compared, evaluated and paid in an equitable manner with like jobs within the same Job Category.

THE METHOD

Updated by Ray Temple

Components

The Temple System Guide Chart Job Evaluation Method (The Method) is made up of the following four components:

- Job Categories
- Factors
- Job Descriptions
- Guide Charts

A brief definition of each will be followed by a detailed discussion.

Job Categories –Job Categories are groups of jobs having similar characteristics and labor markets. Like jobs travel in their own orbits with their own kind and do not commingle for either evaluation or pay purposes. For example, Labor, Trades and Crafts, Office Support, and Technician jobs are basically community oriented and hence have locality evaluation and pay identities. Professional, Administrative and Technological, and Supervisory jobs are tied more to job content and less to community, and hence have national or regional evaluation and pay identities. Job Categories are independent of each other and are only related organizationally – not through and evaluation system which is similar for all jobs.

Factors – These elements are common to all jobs and are selected for measurement. The measurable elements in all jobs, if listed, could total several dozen. However, for most evaluation systems, only a handful are usually considered. These elements can be described in gross terms and are applied to all jobs in many systems. However, in The Method, only five basic Factors, (including a total of 17 sub-elements), are used. Further, since a number of Job Categories are considered, Factor definitions are specifically tailored to each Job Category. The Method provides for Factor definitions adapted to individual Job Categories to achieve maximum relevance in the evaluation process. The Factors are weighted within each Job Category in order to capture the most critical element in each job.

Job Descriptions – There needs to be a formalized way to document job content. In most organizations, a job description accomplishes this. Job documentation is used to evaluate job content, provide objective criteria for making pay comparisons, ensure that jobs are classified according to content as opposed to individual personalities, effectively communicate the job duties to both supervisors and employees, and help the organization defend itself against charges of discrimination. Who should write job descriptions? That will depend on the resources available to the organization, but they should always be reviewed by line management.

Through The Method, a job description:

- Follows a standardized format using common terminology
- Is a working definition of the job
- Allows one job to be measured against other jobs in the same job category
- Gives the client an organizational breakdown so that they can visualize the organization and address changes
- Identifies competition

Guide Charts – These are used to indicate quantitative values for qualitative judgments in the evaluation process. Factor statements are identified with Guide Chart definitions to arrive at relative rankings of jobs, Factor by Factor, and in total. The Guide Charts are defined and adapted specifically to each Job Category for accuracy and are weighted differently to reflect the essence of jobs.

The Factors, Job Descriptions and Guide Charts use common language for each Job Category which reflect the structure and the mission of an organization. This means each set of four components briefly identified herein is tailored for each organization and designed to yield high correlations and internal alignments.

Job Categories

All jobs are identified, and associated, with like jobs in the private sector. Frequently, this is also found in the public sector. Like jobs means jobs that have sufficiently similar characteristics that they can be logically grouped together. The characteristics most usually thought of are:

- Similar levels of formal education as a requirement for entry
- Similar families of jobs
- Similar processes for acquiring skill or proficiency
- Similar processes for qualifying for advancement
- Similar labor markets from which the workers are drawn
- Similar pay relationships

In both the public and private sectors, jobs have traditionally been grouped by blue collar, white collar, and management, just to name the most common segregation. In larger corporations, and in many particular industries, the groupings are more sophisticated, i.e., Professional, Office Support, Supervisory, etc.

The Method groups jobs into a number of Job Categories as described herein. Not all need to be used. Organization size, practically and cost of administration are among the reasons that may dictate how many of the identified Job Categories are actually used.

1. **Labor, Trades and Crafts (LTC)** – These jobs are most commonly unionized; have relatively limited levels of required formal education; are most usually learned on-the-job or through apprenticeship; have relatively short learning times (except in the apprentices able trades); are based on locality patterns for both pay and supply and demand; and advancement is usually based on learning significantly different and progressively more difficult skills. The job families for these jobs are usually comprised of only two or three skill levels.

2. **Office Support and Technicians (OST)** – These jobs may be unionized; have a formal education level commonly identified as high school or completion of 12th grade or post-high school vocational training; are most usually learned on-the-job; have relatively short learning times (except in post high school vocational training); are based on locality patterns for both pay and supply and demand; and advancement is usually based on job modification and ability to do the more difficult tasks within the job family rather than learning specifically different skills as in LTC. The job families normally have two to four skill levels.

3. **Professional, Administrative, Technological (PAT)** – These jobs are normally not unionized; require a baccalaureate level of formal education or work experience at a level equal to the education requirement (normally two years of professional level experience can be equated to one year of college level education); duties are related to subject matter education and application of principles and theories of subject matter; learning time is extended; pay is based on national or regional patterns and supply and demand; advancement is evolutionary, through assumption of progressively more difficult assignments and exercise of judgment; decision making is related to duties and

consequences of action; accountability is clearly defined; the job families normally have three to four (sometimes five in engineering and accounting) skill levels.

Note: Technological is defined as application of theory and principles; duties are directly related to an end product – not supportive as with the technicians.

4. **Protective Occupations, Law Enforcement (POLE)** – These jobs are most commonly unionized; normally require at least 12th grade formal education with a strong effort to require a two year law enforcement course leading to an Associate Degree; duties are either learned on-the-job or through application of formal education; graduation from an academy (police or fire) leads to direct application of this training; the learning period is not long for the normal set of duties; much specialized formal training is normal; these jobs are based on regional patterns for both pay and supply and demand; advancement is through examination in a paramilitary type of organization structure; the job families commonly have two or four levels and then movement is into a supervisory position within the para-military structure.

Note: The duties performed are normally a combination of the duties found in LTC, OST and PAT job categories

5. **Supervisors, Administrators, Managers (SAM)** – These jobs are rarely unionized; normally require a level of formal education which ranges from 12th grade completion through an advanced college level degree depending upon both Job Category supervised and level of job in the supervisory hierarchy; learning time is long and based upon level within the organization; duties are most commonly learned on-the-job; advancement is dependent upon progression to a job of broader responsibility within an organization and is at a

slower rate than in any of the other Job Categories; duties performed are "add-on" skills not directly related to the Job Categories or job families supervised; pay is normally based on national patterns; normally there are three to eight levels within.

6. **Special Occupations (SO)** – These include specific occupations which are characterized by total unionization (in the broad sense of the word); restricted supply; national pay structures; very precise educational requirements; limited advancement opportunities; usually two to four skill levels within the job family. The occupational job families included in this Job Category are:

- Doctors, Dentists, Veterinarians
- Research Scientists
- Attorneys
- Nurses
- Teacher

These job families are treated separately because:

- Their evaluation might place them outside the normal range of PAT Guide Charts, or
- They are linked to health services and hence are a one industry occupation, or
- They are under the control of school districts or other educational organizations with their own unique local hierarchy and evaluation concepts

Factors

Among the list of job characteristics which one could measure for the purpose of job evaluation, five have been selected. These, together with their sub-elements, encompasses the range of elements most often considered when determining relative worth of jobs, one to another. In The Method, each set of five Factors is defined to fit the needs of both the Job Category and the needs of the organization. For example, Factor definitions for very large organizations having a high degree of specialization in many jobs would be different from Factor definitions for a small organization with many mixed jobs. The Factors for LTC, OST, PAT, POLE and SO are:

Job Requirements: This measures the level of knowledge and skills required to perform the duties of the job. This is "going in" knowledge brought by the employee either in the form of academic training or skill and/or adroitness. This can be either manual or mental. Three sub-elements are considered.

a. *Amount* of knowledge or skill in terms of quantity or "how much", i.e., ability to read and write, or skill in operation of a 10 speed truck-trailer rig.
b. *Breadth* of knowledge or skill in terms of variety or "types needed", i.e., knowledge of accounting and auditing principles or skill in use of hand tools.
c. *Depth* of knowledge or skill in terms of "degree of comprehension". i.e., a working knowledge or mastery of subject matter.

Difficulty of Work: This measures what is presented in the performance of work in terms of its relative complexity and the level of judgment, originality, initiative or other mental demands required. Four sub-elements are considered.

a. *Variety* of duties (jobs are composed of duties which are made up of a variety of tasks performed sequentially), i.e., typing, filing, data input and record keeping duties each of which is made up of several tasks.

b. Types and frequency of *problems* in terms of level of complexity and inter-relationships, i.e., identification of client needs to a body of regulations, or interpretation of input data to fit a specific accounting system.

c. *Intensity* in terms of types of judgment which must be made, originality of approach to problems or creativity needed to service clients, i.e., matching up orphans and adopting parents or problem solving within a computer program.

d. *Magnitude* in terms of scope of jurisdiction as related to situations and problems, i.e., planning recreational facilities at the County vs. at the State level.

Responsibility: This measures the impact of the job on results, and the extent to which the job can affect results considering:

a. *Significance* of results on others in terms of the difference that is made by the effort expended, i.e., making the decision to approve a job evaluation or processing a payment in time to take advantage of a discount.

b. The *impact* on scope of work in terms of effort expended, i.e., action taken which affects all retarded children's education in the community or maintaining correspondence logs within a single office of 40 people.

c. Extent of *freedom* in decision-making or ability to act independently in terms of finality of action vs. only recommending a course of action, i.e., daily approving vouchers for payment or recommending action to be taken on an appeal of a claim.

d. The supervisory *controls* over work performed in terms of receiving the objective to be achieved or receiving specific guidance for each step of a process, i.e., being told to audit a system to determine if it meets requirements or being led through each phase of an audit under direct supervisory overview.

Personal Relationships: This measures the interaction of the employee with others both internal and external to the organization. The sub-elements considered are:

a. The *extent* and *frequency* of contacts in terms of time devoted to this aspect of work, i.e., a receptionist vs. a planner who collects data in a community and presents it at annual meetings.
b. The *level* of contacts in terms of interface with peers, supervisors or subordinates during the execution of work, i.e., a financial clerk vs. a budget officer for the entire organization.
c. The *nature* of the contacts in terms of either giving and receiving information, coordinating or interpreting data, or problem solving, i.e., the receptionist vs. a case worker in social services.

The Environment: This measures special or unusual requirements or conditions which are an inherent part of the job and are significant enough to be measured in determining total worth. Sub-elements to be considered are:

a. *Physical* demands in terms of lifting, standing, working in confined space, manual or visual dexterity, and acuity, i.e., stocking material weighing 50 or more pounds vs. the dispatcher who cannot leave the work area except for brief periods of time.
b. *Hazard* in terms of exposure to injury or loss of life, i.e., a machinist vs. attendant in a correctional or penal institution.

c. *Working conditions* at the work site ranging from the pleasant, air-conditioned office to being outdoors in all types of weather, i.e., the secretary vs. the patrol officer on a regular beat either on foot or in a vehicle.

In some of the Special Occupations Job Category, another Factor has to be considered. While basically the Special Occupations are in the PAT Job Category and hence can be evaluated by PAT Factors, there is the Factor of what is commonly called "Rank in the Person". In certain occupations, the basic skills are applied at all levels of the job family. What is added at the higher levels is that which is identified as "added skill" gained not through new knowledge, but in the *application* of existing knowledge. It is a question of how application is made. When it is commonly recognized that through considerable experience and effort an individual has achieved *expertise*, such as status is recognized as "rank" among peers. This is true in the medical, legal and scientific fields particularly. This Factor is in the PAT Guide Chart. Since this applies only to a very limited set of jobs, it is not discussed further.

The Factors for Supervisors, Administrators, Managers (SAM) jobs are quite different. What needs to be measured are "add-on" skills which become a plus factor. The previously discussed Factors are replaced by:

Supervisory Functions:

- Planning
- Organizing
- Budgeting
- Directing
- Instructing
- Setting Standards
- Reviewing
- Training
- Counseling and Disciplining

- Appraising Performance
- Performing Other Personnel Functions

Supervisory Accountability: This seeks to identify and measure the depth and breadth of responsibility and authority to carry out short and long term goals and programs. The degree to which the SAM is held accountable for successful achievement of mission is as important as the execution of the supervisory functions.

Scope of Operations: This is expressed in terms of the number of people directly and indirectly supervised. It is recognized that the larger and more complex the organization supervised, the greater the requirement for coordination, internal interface and internal management. Size alone creates situations and problems which must be effectively and efficiently managed in order to be responsive to the clients served external to the organizational unit.

Job Descriptions

A job description is a formalized way to document job content. This is a process which involves collecting and evaluating relevant information about jobs. Any data collected should:

- Clarify the nature of the work being performed (essential tasks, duties, and responsibilities)
- The level of the work being performed
- The extent and types of knowledge, skill, mental and physical effort and requirements
- Responsibility required for the work being performed

Under The Method this is **job analysis,** or a process to identify and determine in detail the particular job's essential functions and the relative importance of each for a given job.

An important concept to remember is that the analysis is conducted of the job, NOT the person in the job. Job analysis data is collected from incumbents or employees in the job through a **job analysis questionnaire,** but the product of this analysis is a description of the job, not a description of the person.

Under The Method things begin with the basics. It says that a **job** is a collection of tasks and responsibilities that an employee is responsible to conduct. Jobs have titles. A **task** is typically defined as a unit of work, that is, a set of activities needed to produce some result. Complex positions in an organization may include a large number of tasks, which are often referred to as **essential functions.**

The purpose of job analysis is to establish and document the *job relatedness* of employment procedures such as training, selection, compensation/classification, and performance appraisal. The purpose of job analysis is also to meet compliance requirements established by the Americans with Disabilities Act (ADA) under which employers must provide reasonable accommodation to a qualified person with a covered disability. A qualified person is one who, with or without reasonable accommodation, can perform the essential functions of a job. Typically, an essential function meets the following test:

- Is a primary, fundamental purpose of the job
- Is actually performed
- If removed, would fundamentally alter the job
- Usually occupies a large percentage of time
- Can require special expertise or skills

An essential function is identified by percentage of time spent on the function, as well as levels of importance and difficulty.

A job analysis will also look at knowledge, skills and abilities, minimum education and experience requirements, job requirements, equipment used, and environment, as well as the physical and mental/cognitive requirements for the essential functions.

Under The Method, a typical method of job analysis is to give the employee in the job a questionnaire to complete. This is reviewed by their supervisor and then used to draft a job description for review by the employee and/or supervisor. Input from these reviews would be used to finalize the job descriptions.

Preparation of Uncommon Job Descriptions

There are some special situations which may lend themselves to different approaches in the preparation of Job Descriptions. Since each job in an organization must have its own Job Description, the following suggestions can be considered:

a. *Mixed jobs:* These jobs have function/duties which not only may encompass more than one skill level but also commingle job families. In preparing the Job Description, list the functions requiring the highest skills. In that way the job will be evaluated at the highest Job Requirements/Essential Functions and Difficulty levels and will not be under evaluated.

b. *Either/or jobs with same duties:* These are jobs that have a relatively long list of functions, all in the same job family, and can be evaluated at the same level of effort. In preparing the Job Description, include the statement that all or any combination of functions will result in the same evaluation. Then, several secretaries, for example, can all be included in the same job. Obviously, if one secretary job has a function which results in a different total evaluation, a separate Job Description would be required.

c. *Either/or jobs with different functions:* These are jobs in the same job family which have differing functions but all evaluate exactly the same, hence are at the same skill level. For example, in the Accounting Clerk job family, payroll clerk and travel voucher clerk may be included. Write the Job Description stating that either the payroll functions or the travel voucher functions can be performed and the evaluation will be the same.

d. *Multiple jobs:* These are very heavily populated jobs all containing the same functions at the same level. Since they are all equal, one Job Description can do for all. For example, 20 stores clerks and 15 customer services representatives.

The end result is a Job Description for each job and each employee in the organization. That is, each employee prepared Job Analysis Questionnaire will be used to prepare an individual Job Description for each employee.

Other Items to Include

In the Factors discussion on each Job Description, the following should be included, if pertinent:

a. Under Job Requirements, state any required licenses such as a driver's license, nurse's license, etc.

b. Under Job Requirements, indicate any trade-off of pertinent work experience for formal education. Frequently, two years of pertinent experience is equivalent to one year of college.

c. Under Responsibility, specifically state if one "leads" other workers and the nature of this activity.

d. Under Environment, list the weight and frequency with which items are to be lifted, if this is a part of the job. Fifty pounds or over is considered to be heavy and under 25 pounds is considered light.
e. Special skills should be high-lighted under Job Requirements, i.e., the delivery truck driver who drives a semi-truck periodically when asked to delivery large items from the warehouse.
f. While Environment is normally of little impact in establishing the evaluation of PAT jobs, it should be mentioned whenever it is important, i.e., building inspectors frequently are exposed to hazards and weather, hence this Factor may add value to the job in the evaluation process.

NOTE: The Americans with Disabilities Act (ADA) does require adding or expanding information identified in a Job Description. Be sure you are aware of these requirements before developing Job Descriptions.

Guide Charts

The Guide Charts are the basic evaluation tools and are individualized for each Job Category. In number they are as many as are needed for consideration of all the Factors and their sub-elements in the evaluation process. Guide Charts contain varying degrees of Factor sub-elements with numeric values for each degree. They are designed to give the evaluator a quantitative value for each degree, and for a subjective judgment about the relative worth of jobs one to another. The Guide Charts can be validated through analysis of the internal alignment resulting from their use.

A more detailed interpretation of each of the Job Category Guide Charts follows. The Guide Chart for the LTC Category is provided at the end of this section to provide you with an example of how the charts are structured and used.

Labor, Trades and Crafts Guide Chart (LTC)

FACTOR I: *Skills and Knowledge – Skills –* The performance of a task requires the completion of a series of steps usually in sequence. The "least" degree, therefore, is a series of steps which result in a single task done over and over with a minimum of dexterity and effort. A duty of washing windows consists of such tasks as applying a cleaning agent and/or water and removing this from the window. The process is repeated until the duty is completed. The tasks include collecting the equipment needed, applying the cleaning agent and removing it. The steps or actions include such items as placing a ladder or stool in position, immersing a sponge or cloth in a cleaning agent or spraying the cleaning agent on the window, using a squeegee or cloth or tissue to remove the cleaning agent, and moving on to the next window. Obviously, there may be other steps. This example illustrates the process of identifying the steps or actions making up a task which is part of learned skills performed with a minimum of dexterity.

Under this factor, standardized tasks normally can be executed one way or where the variations of execution are few and basically identical or similar. The term "moderately complex" refers to the degree above "simple" or is defined as requiring the execution of a series of steps or actions, which are both sequentially interrelated and require completion of all of them in order to complete the task. As an example, consider assembling a metal bookcase made up of vertical supports, shelves and cross braces, all held together by varying lengths of bolts and nuts. The steps which are sequentially performed are identifying the appropriate vertical support, the corner of the shelf to be attached, the correct length of bolt, the correct size of nut, and the connection of all of these items in the

24

correct order. The entire operation or process is standardized and is considered moderately complex because a series of choices or selections must be made as well as executed in the correct sequence.

As the number of tasks, and the steps executed to complete those increases, the work becomes more complex and varied.

However, the basic guide is the level of effort within the job family. Entry level jobs cannot be correctly identified as being in a degree of complex and varied, if the job family also contains journey and senior level jobs. The degrees are therefore useful in job structuring to arrive at a job family.

The highest degree is defined as consisting of highly complex as well as varied, non-standardized tasks or processes. A master mechanic who is called upon to operate a variety of equipment is a typical example.

Knowledge – The level of learned information, either through formal instruction, observation, or experience, is what is considered. The "least" situation is comprehension of oral instruction and experience in using simple hand tools. The window washing example is typical.

The comprehension of written instructions raises the level of knowledge to one of understanding processes as compared to steps within tasks. From this, one progresses to the capability of interpretations and a variety of interrelated knowledge or experience used to accomplish work.

The highest level of knowledge is evidenced by the ability to be creative, adaptive and judgmental in accomplishing work. This requires a broad range of specialized knowledge such as mathematics and a variety of work processes or actions.

FACTOR II: *Responsibility – Complexity* – This factor measures responsibility as it is related to the Skills and Knowledge required to perform assigned duties. At the lowest degree, the level of accuracy is small and the accountability for materials and equipment low. Since these are minimal and basic, they have low monetary value, hence low responsibility.

At the other extreme where complex, non-standardized tasks are performed, the responsibility for accuracy and its association with materials and equipment of significant value is high. The preponderance of jobs, of course, fall into a broad middle band.

In all three instances, it is assumed the duties are executed, so responsibility for completing the work is a "given." As examples, the window washer is at one end of the scale and the master mechanic at the other end.

Decision Making and Judgment – the freedom to perform work is directly correlated to the nature and amount of supervision received. The greater the latitude to work independently, the greater the responsibility for completing work assignments, including using judgment to make decisions. It is here that thought is also given to the quality of the work performed.

Scope of Work – A third dimension is looked at because of its very close relationship to the other two sub-elements. Scope of Work here refers to the amount of a total work process for which responsibility is herein vested. If maintaining a building is a total work process, then cleaning the building is one operation and washing windows, as contrasted to vacuuming and dusting is a portion of the operation. Note: The missing degrees of this sub-element of the factor are omitted because, by definition, they do not exist.

FACTOR III: *Physical Effort – Frequency and Duration* – The expenditure of effort to get work done is related to the tasks themselves. With this factor, it is a "given" that Factors I and II are present and measured. Now we measure what it takes in expenditure of energy, and for what periods of time, in order to complete the tasks.

Things, for the most part, move in unison. As an example, a plumber's helper, which describes an entry level job, does the bulk of the heavy lifting, holding, crouching, etc. for longer periods of time than the master plumber, who plans and lays out the total plumbing job and makes the vital connections. Hence, entry jobs frequently have higher values on this factor than more senior jobs. As has been indicated, the lifting of 50 or more pounds regularly is in the highest degree.

FACTOR IV: *Working Conditions – Environment* – As might be expected, the circumstances within which work is performed merit measurement in these kinds of jobs. Those jobs which require unusual temperature exposure either inside or out do deserve some consideration in the determination of total value. The starting point is set at what is considered to be reasonable and optimum, such as the environment at one's home or a typical white collar work site.

Hazard – this sub-element directly measures the chances for bodily injury up to death. This is in conjunction with the environment in which the work is performed. The connection is not necessarily direct, i.e., in a machine shop the hazard can be very high, yet the environment may not necessarily be more than the middle position.

Office Support and Technician (OST)

FACTOR I: *Job Requirements and Difficulty of Work – Complexity –* As one moves across the three options, there is an ever-increasing requirement for decision making, in terms of the mental selection of knowledge to complete the tasks or operations. At the lowest degree are found the simplest and least varied series of operations to be performed for task completion. At the other end, all acquired knowledge and experience may be called upon to complete the tasks which may vary with each assignment or duty. The middle position is where the preponderance of jobs are found.

Nature of Acquired Knowledge – What is sought here is the most probable source of knowledge, skill and ability to successfully complete tasks. At the lowest end is found knowledge and skill most usually acquired from relatively brief instruction and on-the-job repetition. For example, punching keys to produce numbers or letters as key punching or typing. The repetition leads to acquired proficiency with minimal errors.

At the other extreme is application of knowledge acquired usually in an academic environment. That is, exposure, through learning from a knowledgeable person the "why" and "how" something occurs in a theoretical sense, so it can be applied in a practical sense. There is a necessity for this knowledge in order to achieve successful completion of tasks. Without this knowledge, it would be either impossible to complete or completion would be by chance.

Amount and Complexity of Knowledge – We are trying here to determine the volume of technical knowledge needed for task completion varying from "terminology" to a full range of specialized information. This does not have to include the entire subject but will incorporate a substantial operating knowledge of a subject. As an example of the "terminology" level of amount, consider a key punch operator who learns and identifies all of the items associated with increases and decreases to an employee's pay during a pay period. At the other extreme, consider the bookkeeping clerk only on "Accounts Payable" who maintains these in ledgers and prepares reports and summaries. These, of course, are an integral part of an accounting system but only a segment must be known and learned for this job.

To use this Chart, jobs are "ranked" before being fitted into subdivisions. The missing degrees are an indication that such situations do not exist, or cannot be found in jobs ranked at either the lowest or highest point.

FACTOR II: *Responsibility* – This is a consideration of 4 elements, broken down as follows.

Opportunity to Make Choices – this is intimately related to the Factor I element of *Complexity of Work* as described above. Where the tasks are simple and repetitive, opportunity to choose what to do to achieve completion is miniscule. At the other end of the scale, choice is continually required in order to achieve completion. The more varied the tasks, the more frequent the opportunity to choose a course of action to be followed.

Usual Consequences of Error – This is the other side of the coin on making choices as expressed in terms of responsibility for actions taken. If, in fact, there is both limited opportunity to make choices and minimum risk or cost if one does make a choice, the responsibility is not heavy. On the other hand, when choices must be made and made correctly in order not to incur excessive costs or waste, responsibility rests heavily on the performer. As a case in point, the Key Punch Operator who omits an item related to an employee's pay either will be corrected by a verifier or in the extreme by the recipient of a pay check. The accounting clerk, who fails to correctly apply State or Federal rules on payroll computation can readily create a costly situation which may take a long time to correct and produce some considerable embarrassment.

Nature of Instructions, Guidelines and Required Judgment – This element seeks to identify the manner work is presented, the amount of available backup information, and the requirement for selection of knowledge from one's own data bank in order to achieve completion of tasks. With precise instruction, either oral or written, and a set of standardized tasks to execute, no real judgment is exercised. The other extreme envisions general instructions, a body of written procedures, and a necessity to think through and make a decision (judgment) on a course of action. This, as well as all other elements of the factor, is in terms of the duties assigned, and their complexity at the level of the job in the hierarchy. A clerical job is not to be denied ranking and points within the nature of the job and its inherent responsibility.

Extent of Supervisory Participation and Control Over Work – There are three choices which can readily be identified as: Close, In Process, and On Conclusion. While it is recognized that this element, more than many of the others, is seen as a continuum, it must not be confused with the performer. That is to say, one who is assigned and completes simple, repetitive tasks, may, it can be argued, move from "close" to "on conclusion" supervisory control. This is not what is being measured here. What we are concerned with is the identification of the normal types of supervisory control needed for task completion by the nature of the tasks themselves, not by the performers. Again, the Key Punch Operator is a case in point. All the work of a Key Punch Operator is normally verified. Therefore, the control is "close" in a case where work is not verified on a machine, it certainly is verified by other means, and frequently. The middle degree says that normally, control is available and exercised sporadically and work is checked upon its completion. The third degree states that inherent in the job is responsibility to be responsive to general guidelines with the end result to be reviewed upon completion.

FACTOR III: *Personal Work Relationships – Nature of Persons Contacted* –This element simply tries to identify the size of the environment within which the job is performed. If, in fact, all work can be successfully completed with contact only within the immediate office or work area, there are fewer requirements than where contacts external to the company, government body or institution, are a normal part of the job.

Purpose and Nature of Required Contacts – Once the extent of contacts are identified, it is necessary to determine why the contacts are required as an inherent part of the job. Three degrees are identified: giving and receiving information *without* interpretation or explanation; informing others via *explanation* or *interpretation* of information, but without responsibility for securing any sort of acceptance or resolution; and finally, informing others without the express intent to secure concurrence or resolve problems, even to the extent of persuasion without coercion.

FACTOR IV: *Physical Effort and Work Environment* – The effort here is to identify the nature of the environment in which work is performed and the personal, physical demands required of the job because of the characteristics of the duties.

Work Environment – The extremes are an optimum work site within which tasks are completed and a hostile work site. Jobs in OST are rarely found in "U" rankings. Inspectors, however, are an example of technicians at this degree. The preponderance of jobs are ranked in "S".

Physical Demands – This element tries to give recognition to bodily demands which are job required for completion of tasks. A Key Punch Operator job is typically at "13" whereas a Store Clerk who normally lifts 50 pounds or more is found in "15".

Professional, Administrative, and Technological (PAT)

Since jobs in this Job Category normally require knowledge acquired in an academic environment (college level), or extensive work experience as a trade-off for formal training, comprehension of theory underlying work techniques and principles is a given.

FACTOR I: *Job Requirements – Nature and extent of Knowledge* – For this element, the distinctions must be made among practical (hands-on), specialized, and broad (across-the-board) knowledge in a given field or occupation. While jobs may be specialized within an occupation, it is expected that above the entry step in this element, there is a general comprehension of the subject matter. An accountant may well specialize in accounts receivable but is expected to know and understand the broader field of accounting. Expertise is not required in the entire field but extensive know-how is expected. Advanced academic work may either be specialized (Criminal Law) or concerned with knowledge of related fields to the specialized subject matter (Public Administration Master's degree after a Business Administration degree). Recognition of the acquisition of practical experience to supplement academic knowledge is given in the middle degree of this element.

Level of Knowledge and Ability Required – Here an effort is made to distinguish between the degrees of comprehension of knowledge, and the extent of original thinking required to complete assigned duties. Degree "3" is the OST structure that qualifies as professional by the nature of duties assigned, i.e., no longer supportive of (as an OST job) but performance within a body of standardized practices and procedures (a personnel interviewer doing only a portion of the whole placement function within a personnel office).

FACTOR II: *Difficulty of Work – Nature of Guidelines* – To measure the mental demands required in completing a set of tasks is difficult. Hence, one has to measure in terms of the nature of guides available (written or oral) and the adaption of this given set of data to the task at hand. Discretion exists, but not to the extreme of "reinventing the wheel." Innovation and interpretation is done within the framework of knowledge available. There is a strong correlation between this element and the *Nature and Extent of Knowledge Complexity of Assigned Work.*

In *Nature and Extent of Knowledge Complexity of Assigned Work,* one measures the intricacies of the tasks, not the variety of the tasks. The options and variables available are what add up to complexity. While it is not suggested that there is "nothing new under the sun," care must be exercised to insure that full use is being made of all available knowledge and precedents. The number and variety of sources which must be sought out add to complexity, but diminish the need for original thinking. A severe human relations problem with complex psychological implications may well be a recognized classic textbook case. It is the effort leading to the resolution of the problem that indicates the complexity, and not necessarily the symptoms of the problem.

FACTOR III: *Responsibility – Impact of Work* – This scale measures the degree to which action taken impacts the purpose and goals of an organization. The question to be answered is whether it really matters if there is successful achievement of tasks and duties assigned to a job vis-à-vis its host organization or programs. The range is from impact on an individual basis to significant influence on major programs and objectives. Within job families, the higher the level of effort the greater the influence of the job upon the organization. This is reflected in the rankings given on the previous factors and illustrates the close correlation among the factors.

Supervisor Participation and Control – As can be observed, freedom to act independently ranges from specific direction with no authority or opportunity for independent thinking, to the least structured situation where the end result is agreed upon, and the means for attainment open. This Chart definitely is ranked on the diagonal. Care must be taken to see the job in its entirely and in its true position within the hierarchy. Independence of action means that performance can only be measured in terms of end results.

FACTOR IV: *Personal Relationship – Scope of Work Contacts* – A range, from contact within a single entity, to contact within a broad universe, exists. Impact of work performed, can and does vary with interaction. Contrary to other Charts, jobs are not necessarily found along a diagonal continuum on this factor. The use of "R" on low level PAT jobs is not uncommon. What is significant is the reason for the interaction which is measured vertically.

Nature and Purpose: Three situations are indicated. The exchange of information without actual use of such is found in low level PAT jobs and an "R 17" rating is possible. Interpretation of data for purposes of rendering service can also be found at any of the horizontal degrees. Care must be exercised that true coordination/interpretation is present and does *not* rely on data or information. The problem solving position connotes responsibility for end results or successful completion or resolution of problems. This does not mean that it is necessary to obtain enthusiastic support of the end result, only acquiescence. Here again, a "N 10" ranking is possible as well as a "R 19".

FACTOR V: *Physical Effort and Work Environment* –This factor is almost never skill level determining. However, it is sometimes necessary to give recognition to unusual or undesirable environments or excessive physical demands. As can be seen, in the preponderance of jobs, no point value is assigned because an "S" value is normally assumed. However, wherever or whenever the situation arises that job requirements exceed "S", recognition should properly be given.

Supervisory and Managerial (SAM)

These Guide Charts which cover the three SAM Factors are designed to cover the "add-on" elements which characterize those skills and responsibilities over and above the Factors inherent in a non-supervisory position in LTC, OST, or PAT jobs. The assumption is made that a Supervisor has at least "journey" level proficiency over the jobs directed. Therefore, it is the value of supplemental skills and responsibilities which is to be measured.

FACTOR I: *Supervisory Functions – Planning –* If present, identify and distinguish among day-to-day, short, and long term planning related exclusively to successful achievement of work and program goals. Approval by higher supervisory levels is assumed. Where present, coordination among lower level Supervisors is expected.

Organizing – Here methodology in accomplishing planned effort is identified. Common items worked upon are utilization of staff for maximum efficiency, team development and work flow through the unit. Methods and procedures for efficient task completion are under constant review at the highest degree of this element.

Budgeting – This element is dependent, for its point value, on the impact of coordination from lower level Supervisors, developing justifications, and defending the requests before the highest levels necessary. This may be in person or in writing with maximum credit given to submittals which are basically unchanged by superiors. Thus, responsibility for documentation becomes vested in the job being evaluated.

Directing – This measures the process of work assignment to subordinates or lower level Supervisors and the balancing of staff against workload and completion dates. There is distinct responsibility for effective utilization of resources through active direction and leadership. This is the "What-to-do" part of the job.

Instructing – This is a measurement of "How-to-do" through oral or written documentation of procedure and guides. With lower level Supervisors, there is a responsibility for granting approval of their instructions.

Setting Standards – The determination of what is acceptable work and what is not calls for the development of yardsticks as measuring tools. The use and interpretation of these standards or yardsticks is inherent in a supervisory job.

Reviewing – Here the standards previously established are reviewed against actual output to determine if completed work is acceptable. This is closely related to both Standards development and instructing. Successful work completion depends on all three.

Training – This is formal development instruction designed to assure longer term skill acquisition, either in a specific area or in inter-related areas, and is differentiated from *Instructing* which is a hands-on process. The *Training* element concerns itself with the broader picture of how to get the job done rather than how to complete a specific task as in instructing.

Counseling and Disciplining – Here the day-to-day inter-relationships between Supervisors and employees are measured. The responsibility for maintaining a level of behavior consistent with rules and regulations involves discipline as well as guidance.

Appraising Performance – Once standards of acceptable performance for task completion have been established, it is possible to appraise accomplishment. This should be both an on-going activity and a periodic one-on-one review. When other levels of supervision are present or involved, review and coordination are required.

Performing Other Personnel Functions – Since the Supervisor or Manager is really the operating personnel representative in day-to-day activities, there may be a range of these responsibilities, depending upon the delegation granted by the organization's Personnel Manager. This element measures these delegations.

FACTOR II: *Supervisory Accountability* – This Factor seeks to determine the degree of accountability for the quality of end product turned out. Whereas Factor I is concerned with the Supervisor-employee relationship and the responsibilities inherent therein, here the emphasis is on Supervisor-superior relationships. This varies with delegation. The freedom to act, the independence to make decisions and the extent of supervisory control all make up the level of the job within the hierarchy. Hence, the highest degree is associated with correspondingly higher organization levels than the lowest degree.

FACTOR III: *Scope of Work Operations* – There is a built in interrelationship between size or number of employees supervised and the number of problems which require resolution in order to achieve acceptable output. With less than three others to direct, the relationship tends to be that of a "working leader" rather than a true Supervisor. Normally, when 75% or more of a worker's time is devoted to actual hands on task completion related to end product, there is no true supervisory responsibility. When at least half of one's time is devoted to the Factor I elements, supervisory responsibility has emerged. As the number of employees for whom responsibility exists increases, the number and level of intermediate Supervisors increases. The responsibility then changes to one of coordination with greater emphasis on planning on a broader basis. This is also related to Factor II since the accountability increases.

To provide you with a better picture on how a guide chart functions and is used to determine internal values we are offering the following. It is the LTC Guide Chart minus the Point Value Sheet which contains the actual point values for each factor.

LTC GUIDE CHART SAMPLE

LTC Scoring Sheet

JOB TITLE:

Place an X in the [   ] next to the selected answer, making only one selection per factor.

Factor I: Skills and Knowledge

[   ] A1   [   ] A2   [   ] A3   [   ] B1   [   ] B2

[   ] B3   [   ] B4   [   ] C2   [   ] C3   [   ] C4

[   ] D2   [   ] D3   [   ] D4

Factor I Point Value =

Factor II: Responsibility

[   ] E1   [   ] E2   [   ] E3   [   ] E4   [   ] E5

[   ] F1 [   ] F2   [   ] F3   [   ] F4   [   ] F5

[   ] F6   [   ] F7 [   ] G1   [   ] G2   [   ] G3

[   ] G4   [   ] G5

Factor II Point Value =

Factor III: Physical Effort

[ ] H1   [ ] H2   [ ] H3   [ ] I1   [ ] I2

[ ] I3   [ ] J1   [ ] J2   [ ] J3

Factor III Point Value =

Factor IV: Working Conditions

[ ] K1   [ ] K2   [ ] K3   [ ] K4   [ ] L1

[ ] L2   [ ] L3   [ ] L4   [ ] M1   [ ] M2

[ ] M3   [ ] M4

Factor IV Point Value =

Name of Supervisor Completing Scoring Sheet

Point assessment and final review conducted by: Total
Point Value:

Labor, Trades and Crafts (LTC)

Guide Chart

Directions: To evaluate jobs assigned to the LTC job category, you will use this Guide Chart and the LTC Scoring Sheet. It is also recommended that you refer to the current job description for the position to verify your decisions. Do not write on the Guide Chart. Record your answers on the Scoring Sheet. You will complete a separate Scoring Sheet for each job identified for the LTC category.

As you look at the statements under each factor, select the one statement that best identifies how you would describe its relationship to the job. Record your decision by turning to the LTC Scoring Sheet and placing an X in the [   ] by your answer.

Factor I: Skills and Knowledge

A1: This work consists of simple repetitive tasks and operations. Ability to follow simple oral instructions; understand general work processes, have practical knowledge of use of hand tools.

A2: This work consists of simple repetitive tasks and operations. Ability to read and write at an elementary level; understands work processes, methods and use of equipment and machinery.

A3: This work consists of simple repetitive tasks and operations. Thorough knowledge of one trade or working knowledge of a variety of trades; ability to interpret work instructions and other technical guides; reads blueprints; practical knowledge of tools, machinery and equipment; some work planning and layout; practical shop mathematics.

B1: This work consists of moderately complex, relatively *standardized* tasks, processes or operations. Ability to follow simple oral instructions; understands general work processes; has practical knowledge of use of hand tools.

B2: This work consists of moderately complex, relatively *standardized* tasks, processes or operations. Ability to read and write at an elementary level; understands work processes, methods and use of equipment and machinery.

B3: This work consists of moderately complex, relatively *standardized* tasks, processes or operations. Thorough knowledge of one trade or working knowledge of a variety of trades; ability to interpret work instructions and other technical guides; reads blueprints, practical knowledge of tools, machinery and equipment; some work planning and layout; practical shop mathematics.

B4: This work consists of moderately complex, relatively *standardized* tasks, processes or operations. Ability to use memory, judgment and ingenuity in planning and layout work; skill in using variety of equipment and machinery; plans and lays out work; practical knowledge of variety of related skills including shop mathematics to level of geometry and trigonometry.

C2: This work consists of complex varied *standardized* tasks, processes, or operations. Ability to read and write at an elementary level; understands work processes, methods and use of equipment and machinery.

C3: This work consists of complex varied *standardized* tasks, processes, or operations. Thorough knowledge of one trade or working knowledge of a variety of trades; ability to interpret work instructions and other technical guides; reads blueprints; practical knowledge of tools, machinery and equipment; some work planning and layout; practical shop mathematics.

C4: This work consists of complex varied *standardized* tasks, processes or operations. Ability to use memory, judgment and ingenuity in planning and layout work; skill in using variety of equipment and machinery; plans and lays out work; practical knowledge of variety of related skills including shop mathematics to level of geometry and trigonometry.

D2: This work consists of highly complex varied *non-standardized* tasks, processes or operations. Ability to read and write at an elementary level; understands work processes, methods and use of equipment and machinery.

D3: This work consists of highly complex varied *non-standardized* tasks, processes or operations. Thorough knowledge of one trade or working knowledge of a variety of trades; ability to interpret work instructions and other technical guides; reads blueprints, practical knowledge of tools, machinery and equipment; some work planning and layout; practical shop mathematics.

D4: This work consists of highly-complex varied *non-standardized* tasks, processes or operations. Ability to use memory, judgment and ingenuity in planning and layout work; skill in using variety of equipment and machinery; plans and lays out work' practical knowledge of variety of related skills including shop mathematics to level of geometry and trigonometry.

Factor II: Responsibility

E1: Work - simple repetitive action, simple work sequences, low degree of accuracy required, low degree of care and skill required to prevent damage to tools. Work performed under close supervision. Work instructions and complete and specific. No authority to deviate from instructions. Works on only a portion of an operation which is part of a work process.

E2: Work – simple repetitive action, simple work sequences, low degree of accuracy required, low degree of care and skill required to prevent damage to tools. Work performed under moderate supervision. Instructions are relatively complete. Applies knowledge of technical manuals and work precedents. Recommends or requests deviations from general instructions when necessary. Works on an operations which is part of a total work process; planning and layout responsibilities not extensive.

E3: Work – simple repetitive action, simple work sequences, low degree of accuracy required, low degree of care and skill required to prevent damage to tools. Work performed under moderate supervision. Instructions are relatively complete. Applies knowledge of technical manuals and work precedents. Recommends or requests deviations from general instructions when necessary. Works on only a portion of an operation which is part of a work process.

E4: Work – simple repetitive action, simple work sequences, low degree of accuracy required, low degree of care and skill required to prevent damage to tools. Work performed under moderate supervision. Instructions are relatively complete. Applies knowledge of technical manuals and work precedents. Recommends or requests deviations from general instructions when necessary. Works on an operation which is part of a total work process, planning and layout responsibilities not extensive.

E5: Work – simple repetitive action, simple work sequences, low degree of accuracy required, low degree of care and skill required to prevent damage to tools. Work performed under moderate supervision. Instructions are relatively complete. Applies knowledge of technical manuals and work precedents. Recommends or requests deviations from general instructions when necessary. Works on a total work process, responsibility for planning and layout inherent in job; advises others on practical aspects of work sequences and techniques.

F1: Work – moderately complex, involved in relatively varied tasks. Moderate degree of accuracy required. Moderate degree of care and skill required to protect tools, materials, and prevent injury to others. Work performed under close supervision. Work instructions are complete and specific. No authority to deviate from instructions. Works on only a portion of an operation which is part of a work process.

F2: Work – moderately complex, involved in relatively varied tasks. Moderate degree of accuracy required. Moderate degree of care and skill required to protect tools, materials, and prevent injury to others. Work performed under close supervision. Work instructions are complete and specific. No authority to deviate from instructions. Works on an operation which is part of a total work process; planning and layout responsibilities not extensive.

F3: Works – moderately complex, involved in relatively varied tasks. Moderate degree of accuracy required. Moderate degree of care and skill required to protect tools, materials, and prevent injury to others. Work performed under moderate supervision. Instructions are relatively complete. Applies knowledge of technical manuals and work precedents. Recommends or requests deviations from general instructions when necessary. Works on only a portion of an operation which is part of a work process.

F4 Works – moderately complex, involved in relatively varied tasks. Moderate degree of accuracy required. Moderate degree of care and skill required to protect tools, materials, and prevent injury to others. Work performed under moderate supervision. Instructions are relatively complete. Applies knowledge of technical manuals and work precedents. Recommends or requests deviations from general instructions when necessary. Works on an operation which is part of a total work process; planning and layout responsibilities not extensive.

F5: Works – moderately complex, involved in relatively varied tasks. Moderate degree of accuracy required. Moderate degree of care and skill required to protect tools, materials, and prevent injury to others. Work performed under moderate supervision. Instructions are relatively complete. Applies knowledge of technical manuals and work precedents. Recommends or requests deviations from general instructions when necessary. Works on a total work process; responsibility for planning and layout inherent in job; advises others on practical aspects of work sequences and techniques

G3: Work – responsible for variety of different operations to complete assignments; high degree of accuracy required to protect tools, materials and prevent injury to others. Work performed under moderate supervision. Instructions are relatively complete. Applies knowledge of technical manuals and work precedents. Recommends or requests deviations from general instructions when necessary. Works on only a portion of an operation which is part of a work process.

G4: Work – responsible for variety of different operations to complete assignments; high degree of accuracy required to protect tools, materials and prevent injury to others. Work performed under moderate supervision. Instructions are relatively complete. Applies knowledge of technical manuals and work precedents. Recommends or requests deviations from general instructions when necessary. Works on an operation which is part of a total work process; planning and layout responsibilities not extensive.

G5: Work – responsible for variety of different operations to complete assignments; high degree of accuracy required to protect tools, materials and prevent injury to others. Work performed under moderate supervision. Instructions are relatively complete. Applies knowledge of technical manuals and work precedents. Recommends or requests deviations from general instructions when necessary. Works on a total work process; responsibility for planning and layout inherent in job; advises others on practical aspects of work sequences and techniques.

G6: Work – responsible for variety of different operations to complete assignments; high degree of accuracy required to protect tools; materials and prevent injury to others. Works with considerable independence from supervisory controls. Instructions are general. Has authority to deviate from instructions with prior approval. Make decisions and judgments affecting quality and adequacy of work. Works on an operation which is part of a total work process; planning and layout responsibilities not extensive.

G7: Work – responsible for variety of different operations to complete assignments; high degree of accuracy required to protect tools, materials and prevent injury to others. Works with considerable independence from supervisory controls. Instructions are general. Technical manuals and work precedents may be modified to be practically applies. Has authority to deviate from instructions with prior approval. Make decisions and judgments affecting quality and adequacy of work. Works on a total work process; responsibility for planning and layout inherent in job; advises others on practical aspects of work sequences and techniques.

Factor III: Physical Effort

H1: Effort is exerted for short periods of time. Strain not prolonged. Effort involves light lifting of tools, objects and working material, or light, pushing and pulling, and/or normal visual or hearing acuity. Normally performs in seated or standing position.

H2: Effort is exerted for short periods of time. Strain not prolonged. Effort involves moderate lifting, pushing, pulling, reaching, bending and/or more than normal visual or hearing acuity required for precision work. Performs in an abnormal sitting or standing position. Manual dexterity moderate.

H3: Effort is exerted for short periods of time. Strain not prolonged. Effort involves heavy lifting, pushing or pulling, and excessive crouching, stooping or lying in prone position, and/or involves intense strain on sight or hearing. Performs usually in a non-sitting position. High manual dexterity may be required.

I1: Effort is exerted regularly for sustained periods. Strain may be intense for frequent or moderate duration. Effort involves light lifting of tools, objects and working material, or light pushing and pulling, and/or normal visual or hearing acuity. Normally performs in seated or standing position.

I2: Effort is exerted regularly for sustained periods. Strain may be intense for frequent or moderate duration. Effort involves moderate lifting, pushing, pulling, reaching, bending and/or more than normal visual or hearing acuity required for precision work. Performs in an abnormal sitting or standing position. Manual dexterity moderate.

I3: Effort is exerted regularly for sustained periods. Strain may be intense for frequent or moderate duration. Effort involves heavy lifting, pushing or pulling, and excessive crouching, stooping or lying in prone position and/or involves intense strain on sight or hearing. Performs usually in a non-sitting position. High manual dexterity may be required.

J1: Effort is prolonged and frequent. Strain may be extended in duration. Effort involves light lifting of tools, objects and working material, or light pushing and pulling, and/or normal visual or hearing acuity. Normally performs in seated or standing position.

J2: Effort is prolonged and frequent. Strain may be extended in duration. Effort involves moderate lifting, pushing, pulling, reaching, bending and/or more than normal visual or hearing acuity required for precision work. Performs in an abnormal sitting or standing position. Manual dexterity moderate.

J3: Effort is prolonged and frequent. Strain may be extended in duration. Effort involves heavy lifting, pushing, or pulling, and excessive crouching, stooping, or lying in prone position and/or involves intense strain on sight or hearing. Performs usually in a non-sitting position. High manual dexterity may be required.

Factor IV: Working Conditions

K1: Adequate working conditions with at least minimum environmental conditions to assure the health, safety, and comfort of the workers. Minimum hazardous working conditions.

K2: Adequate working conditions with at least minimum environmental conditions to assure the health, safety, and comfort of the workers. Occasional exposure to hazardous work conditions (noise, fumes, height, slippery, vibration, moving parts).

K3: Adequate working conditions with at least minimum environmental conditions to assure the health, safety, and comfort of the workers. Recurring work conditions which involve chance of injury or loss of life.

K4: Adequate working conditions with at least minimum environmental conditions to assure the health, safety, and comfort of the workers. Daily involvement with work that involves chance of major injury or loss of life.

L1: Moderate exposure to dust, grease, temperature, noise, inadequate lighting, inclement weather, etc. May work where safety or health may be a factor. Minimum hazardous working conditions.

L2: Moderate exposure to dust, grease, temperature, noise, inadequate lighting, inclement weather, etc. May work where safety or health may be a factor. Occasional exposure to hazardous work conditions (noise, fumes, height, slippery, vibration, moving parts).

L3: Moderate exposure to dust, grease, temperature, noise, inadequate lighting, inclement weather, etc. May work where safety or health may be a factor. Recurring work conditions (noise, fumes, height, slippery, vibration, moving parts).

L4: Moderate exposure to dust, grease, temperature, noise, inadequate lighting, inclement weather, etc. May work where safety or health may be a factor. Daily involvement with work that involves chance of major injury or loss of life.

M1: Prolonged and frequent exposure to dust, grease, extreme temperature, or severe outdoor weather conditions. Exposure to unfavorable health or safety conditions frequently present. Minimum hazardous working conditions.

M2: Prolonged and frequent exposure to dust, grease, extreme temperature, or severe outdoor weather conditions. Exposure to unfavorable health or safety conditions frequently present. Occasional exposure to hazardous work conditions (noise, fumes, height, slippery, vibration, moving parts).

M3: Prolonged and frequent exposure to dust, grease, extreme temperature, or severe outdoor weather conditions. Exposure to unfavorable health or safety conditions frequently present. Recurring work conditions which involve chance of injury or loss of life.

M4: Prolonged and frequent exposure to dust, grease, extreme temperature, or severe outdoor weather conditions. Exposure to unfavorable health or safety conditions frequently present. Daily involvement with work that involves chance of major injury or loss of life.

BASE PAY

Pay Philosophy

Before embarking on determining base pay, it is necessary to have an agreement on an organizational pay philosophy. This optimally is written and covers the following elements.

1. **Competitive position in the labor market:** The organization should have a clear understanding of how competitive it wishes to be in the labor market. Does it want to be a leader? Does it want to be a follower? Does it want to be in the middle, the upper quartile, or the middle 50%? Being near the bottom of the pay scale may result in excessive turnover and a less effective labor force. This competitive determination is important because it is the basis for the remaining items discussed below.

2. **In-hiring Policy:** The rate at which workers are hired in relation to the labor market's pay can have significant impact on the organization payroll. It would be made up of pay rates that range from entry levels to long term workers. It also reflects a range of skill levels. On average at any skill level, the typical workers' pay represents about three years' experience at that skill level. A common practice is to in-hire at a minimum that reflects the least an organization is willing to pay to have work done at that skill level, and at the same time the rate at which workers can be recruited. The survey minimum-maximum ranges can be a guide to show at what pay other organizations start workers.

3. **Merit Policy:** It has become a common practice to grant workers an annual pay increase. Unfortunately, this has become a very confused picture in some organizations. Some call this a cost-of-living increase. Some commingle an economic adjustment with length of service adjustments. What is referred to here as a merit increase is an increase (annual or more frequent) granted to a worker for performance above an established norm, i.e., for work which exceeds what is normally expected as a result of the pay granted. This is a true merit increase. It can be granted in one year and not in another. It has nothing to do with "survival", i.e., the completion of a length of time on the job regardless of performance. In a common sense way, there is no reason to grant a pay increase solely for service time. Merit increases normally are earned by about 50% of the workers during any one year. They should be budgeted for and used only with a performance rating system.

4. **Economic Increases:** These are usually given annually and in a pure sense should only represent the increase in the pay range from one year to the next. The reason a pay range rises each year has little to do with the cost of living directly. The pay range goes up (or down) because organizations in the labor market pay workers: higher in-hiring rates, promotional increases for assuming more responsibility, merit increases for better than average performance and what the supply and demand factor in the labor market requires. An annual survey can show the change in the pay range. If an organization decides to raise its workers' pay by the amount the pay range has risen over a year, that is an economic increase not related to either meritorious performance or length of service internally within that organization. It is a reaction to external economic conditions. Such a pay adjustment is recommended in order

to keep an organization's workers "whole" within the established pay philosophy.

5. **Promotion Policy:** It is a well-established practice to grant a worker a pay adjustment whenever that worker is asked to assume more responsibility by performing work evaluated higher that what is presently assigned. This may occur at any time within a year. It is generally rewarded at about twice the rate of a merit increase. An organization may establish rules as to frequency, amount (when added to merit and economic adjustments), and service required between pay adjustments. This increase should be kept separate and apart from both merit (performance) increases and economic adjustments because it portrays what the organization would have to pay if it had to recruit to fill a job instead of promoting an existing worker.

Determining Base Pay

Have you ever wondered how a company decides how much to pay for a particular job? Imagine that you have seen a job posted on the Internet. It reads, "Office Assistant Wanted. Will answer the phone and greet visitors. Some word processing duties. Other duties are assigned. Start at $12.00 per hour." How did the manager decide to pay $12.00 per hour? Why did she decide that was fair? We will now cover the two types of "fairness" important in designing a base pay system. It will also provide an opportunity to review what we have discussed in presenting **The Method,** and how it figures into determining Base Pay.

Internal Equity

The first consideration is that the base pay system needs to be *internally equitable.* This means that the pay differentials between jobs need to be appropriate. The amount of base pay assigned to jobs needs to reflect the relative contribution of each job to the company's business objectives. In determining this, the manager should ask his or herself, "How does the work of the office assistant described above compare with the work of the office manager?" Another question to be asked is, "Does one contribute to solutions for customers more than another?" Internal equity implies that pay rates should be the same for jobs where the work is similar and different for jobs where the work is dissimilar. In addition, determining the appropriate differential in pay for people performing different work is a key challenge. With **The Method** we use two tools to help make these decisions: job analysis and job evaluation.

Job analysis is a systematic method to discover and describe the differences and similarities among jobs. A good job analysis collects sufficient information to adequately identify, define, and describe the content of a job. Since job titles may in and of themselves be misleading, for example "systems analyst" does not reveal much about the job, the content of the job is more important to the analysis than the title. In general, a typical job analysis attempts to describe the skill, effort, responsibility, and working conditions of each job. *Skill* refers to the experience, training, education, and ability required by the job. *Effort* refers to the mental or physical degree of effort actually expended in the performance of the job. *Working conditions* refers to the physical surroundings and hazards of a job, including dimensions such as inside versus outside work, heat, cold, and poor ventilation. A *job description* summarizes the information collected in the job analysis.

Job evaluation is a process that takes the information gathered by the job analysis and places a value on the job; it systematically determines the relative worth of jobs based on a judgment of each job's value to the organization. The most commonly used method of job evaluation is the "point method", i.e., **The Method**. The point method consists of three steps: (1) defining a set of compensable factors, (2) creating a numerical scale for each compensable factor, and (3) weighting each compensable factor. Each job's relative value is determined by the total points assigned to it.

The result of the job analysis and job evaluation processes will be a pay structure in which jobs are ordered by their value to the organization.

Internal Ranking of Jobs

Under **The Method,** just as each Job Category has its own set of Guide Charts, they also have their own pay structures, and the results of the evaluation conducted on each job sets the foundation for each structure.

With the evaluation results we can now *internally rank* all jobs within each Job Category. This is based on the total point value determined through the evaluation. The total point value determines the pay grade for each job. Since each grade also has its own *pay range* we are now taking the first steps in setting in place pay structures for each Job Category.

With the LTC, OST, PAT, and POLE categories there are six (6)grade levels. Using the LTC category for example, here is the breakdown:

600 – 695 points ………………….LTC 6 (highest grade)

500 – 595 points ....LTC 5

400 – 495 points ....LTC 4

300 – 395 points ....LTC 3

200 – 295 points ....LTC 2

100 – 195 points ....LTC 1 (lowest grade)

With the SAM category there are eight (8) classifications:

70 – 79 points .... SAM 8 (highest classification)

60 – 69 points ....SAM 7

50 – 59 points .... SAM 6

40 – 49 points ....SAM 5

30 – 39 points .... SAM 4

20 – 29 points .... SAM 3

10 – 19 points ....SAM 2

0 – 9   points ....SAM 1

External Equity

The second consideration in creating a base pay system is *external equity.* External equity refers to the relationship between one company's pay levels in comparison to what other employers pay. Some employers set their pay levels higher than their competition, hoping to attract the best applicants. This is called "leading the market." The risk in leading the market is that a company's costs will generally be higher than its competitors' costs. Other employers set their pay levels lower than their competitors, hoping to save labor cost. This is called "lagging the market." The risk in lagging the market is that the company will be unable to attract the best applicants. Most employers set their pay levels in the same range as their competition. This is called "matching the market." Matching the market maximizes the quality of talent while minimizing labor costs.

An important question in external equity is how you define your market. Traditionally, markets can be defined in one of three ways. The first way to define your market is by identifying companies who hire employees with the same occupation or skills, such as electrical engineers. A second way to define a market is by identifying companies who operate in the same geographic area. For example, if the company is in Denver, Colorado, the market would be defined as all companies in Denver, Colorado. A third way to define a company's market is by identifying direct competitors, that is, those companies who produce the same products and services. For example, Shady Acres Veterinary Clinic may define its market as all other veterinary clinics. Notice that these three characterizations can interact: Shady Acres might define its market as all veterinary clinics in Denver, Colorado, that employ veterinary technicians.

Once you have defined your market, the next step is to survey the compensation paid by employer in your market. Surveys can be done in a variety of ways. First, there are publicly available data through the Bureau of Labor Statistics in the United States. Second, there are publicly available data through the Internet, from sites such as www.salary.com or www.haypaynet.com. Third, salary information can be obtained from a third party source, such as an industry group or employer organization, which has collected general information for a geographic region or industry. Fourth, the company can hire a consulting organization to custom design a survey. Finally, the company can conduct a survey itself.

Salary Survey

*A **salary survey** is a tool specifically designed for defining a fair and competitive salary for the employees of a company. The survey output is data on the average or median salary for a specific position, taking into consideration the region, industry, company size, etc. Input data is aggregated directly from an employer or employee.*

Types of Salary Surveys by Data Source

Salary surveys are differentiated based on their data source into those that

- obtain data from companies, or
- obtain data from employees.

Salary survey operators strive to obtain the most relevant input data possible. There is no way to generalize which approach is correct. The first option may satisfy large companies, while the second is largely for smaller companies.

Salary surveys based on data from companies

This is the traditional approach where consulting companies obtain survey input data from specific companies. Companies are provided with a wide-ranging questionnaire to gather information about the company and its employees.

Advantages of salary surveys using data from employers

- Long-term experience – these are global companies with long histories in the vast majority of cases.
- Brand recognition – these companies are well-established on the market and have already created a reputation. Brands such as Pay Well (PricewaterhouseCoopers/PwC), AON Hewitt, Mercer and the Hay Group are examples of such companies.
- Consulting activities – given that salary surveys are one of the primary lines of business for these companies, they have consultants on staff who can deliver their consulting expertise in obtaining input data (ensuring data is aggregated using the correct method) and other more wide-ranging consulting activities. Such consulting may include job descriptions, evaluating specific jobs and even the creation of a salary system..
- Detailed catalogue of positions – jobs must be assigned to the correct position during the survey to ensure the compared salary corresponds to the work performed. Positions are described in detail in the survey given the long-term experience and direct connection to parent companies. The same is true of responsibilities, powers and subordinates, and superiority structures, in addition to the actual job description itself.
- They facilitate international salary comparison – international salary comparisons for individual positions are possible given that the operators of these salary surveys are companies with international know-how, and identical methods are applied in dozens of countries around the world.

Disadvantages of salary surveys using data from employers

- Lengthy process of completing the form – time demands are high given the detailed nature of the form used to obtain input data. The questionnaire includes questions that require answers from multiple departments: financial (company profits) and human resources (salaries, numbers of employees, training and education costs, etc.). A company may not answer some questions clearly if it monitors specific indicators in a different structure and if estimates are provided in the questionnaire, which deform the results.
- Partial coverage of the entire market – the goal of any salary survey is to include all types of companies, big and small, domestic and foreign, in various industries, etc. Given that only the companies that buy such a survey are involved, these surveys do not cover the entire labor market. Often they only include large and wealthy industries such as IT, telecommunications, pharmaceuticals, banking, cars, electronics, etc. Other industries such as sales, other industry, construction, etc. are composed of companies that cannot afford such a salary survey, which means their industries are not completely covered.
- Sensitive data – not every company wants to disclose sensitive data on profitability, fluctuations, and employee salaries in any specific form. Survey participants cannot avoid these questions.
- Non-current data – salary surveys based on data from employers aggregate input information over a matter of months. The standard data aggregation period is 3 to 4 months. Processing follows, which may take another 2 months. Companies may only receive the data they need after a half-year delay. The labor market changes over this time, in particular in times of economic growth, and the data is no longer up-to-date after aggregation, processing and evaluation.

- High price – salary surveys based on this approach are expensive. Prices are in the thousands of dollars, depending on if the company is actively involved in the survey or does not participate and only purchases the survey results (more expensive in this case).

Salary surveys based on data from employees

Collecting data from employees primarily refers to the collection of data using the Internet.

Advantages of salary surveys aggregating data from employees

- Large sample of respondents – salaries are of interest to every employee, and providing information about themselves gives the opportunity to compare their current situation with others on the labor market. It is no surprise that these types of salary surveys have a large sample of respondents. Surveys are equipped with technical resources to expose duplicate records, thereby rendering fears of misuse unjustified.
- All types of companies – employees in all types of companies are interested in salaries, regardless of the type of work, region, industry, size, company ownership, etc. Such survey aggregate data from a multitude of different companies.
- Transparency of results – this method provides fast access to the most in-demand information to support decision-making; the information is also transparently depicted and easy to understand.
- Results without providing company data – companies use the results of such surveys without actually providing their own data. This provides an opportunity to exploit information

about the market without concerns over a loss of sensitive data.

- Easy access to the required data –salary surveys of this type are accessible over the Internet. Companies have access to them anywhere with Internet connection: in offices, cafes, hotels, at home, etc.
- Currentness–data is continuously added to this type of survey; the database is propagated with new data on a daily basis with old (year-old) data automatically replaced.
- Financial accessibility – the survey method based on data from employees does not incur the same costs as surveys based on data from employers. These surveys are at a much more accessible price point for this reason. **Small and medium enterprises primarily use this type of survey.**
- Real employee salaries and benefits – surveys based on data from employees are directly connected to the specific positions in which the employees work. The resulting data describes the situation of a specific employee and not the general situation in the company. Companies often declare benefits such as company mobile phones, but in practice an employee may actually only be eligible for such benefit in select positions and after working for the company for at least one year.

Disadvantages of salary surveys aggregating data from employees

- Temporary mistrust in this method – a lack of confidence occurs based on the argument that "people lie on the Internet." Experience has shown that people do not lie but rather complete questionnaires accurately if they want to obtain reliable information from a website. Respondents provide details of their own salary because they are motivated to compare their salary with others. An attempt to provide misleading information is basically lying to oneself.

- Less brand awareness – these salary surveys do not enjoy the same brand recognition as traditional salary surveys, and companies are only starting to have confidence in their results.
- Internet population – this type of survey requires that respondents are computer literate and have Internet access. This leads to an assumption that the structure of respondents correlates to the structure of the Internet population. This population has a lower share of employees with lower levels of education and from smaller communities. This effect is mitigated by the increasing levels of computer literacy and Internet coverage.
- Level of detail of results – survey output data is a reflection of the data provided by the respondents, i.e., company employees. They cannot be asked specific details concerning remuneration as they are asked in surveys using data from companies. The average employee does not know how much education and training activities cost, company revenues, etc. As such, the survey outputs do not provide such detailed data. They are based on the most basic indicators on which salaries depend: position, region, industry, previous experience, education, etc. – all questions the respondents can answer.

Creating Base Pay

SOURCE: SHRM.org

#1: Establish overall pay range

Determine a company minimum and a company maximum pay. The minimum will be for the first and lowest grade and the maximum will be for the last and highest grade. Use a listing of all company positions and current salary survey data relative to those positions to set these parameters and incorporate the company's compensation philosophy to lead, lag or pay at market. (Paying at market means your midpoint will match the average salary for that position; lagging the market will set a midpoint below the average salary for that position; leading the market will set a midpoint above the average salary for that position.)

A pay range will generally spread +/- 15-20% from the midpoint, but any range the employer feels is appropriate is acceptable, and ranges may be different for different grades. For example, if your lowest paid position is an Administrative Assistant and you wish to pay at market, and salary survey data for that position shows an average salary of $25,000, a 15% spread for that job would be $21,250 (min), $25,000 (midpoint) and $28,750 (max), making $21,250 your overall minimum salary. Do the same for the highest paid position to set the overall maximum salary the company is currently willing to pay.

#2: Establish number of grades

Select the number of grades to be used based on the size of the company, job diversity, job evaluation results, etc. Large companies may find it more practical to use more grades, a small company with a CEO, managers who report to the CEO and administrative assistants might have three (3) pay grades. A similar, larger company, perhaps with administrative staff, exempt professionals, supervisors, managers, directors and chiefs, may have six (6) pay grades. An international company may have more than one pay grade system to reflect geographical differences. There is no one right number of pay grades; choose the number that makes most sense for your organization and its structure. Typically, however, the number of pay grades will depend on the size of your organization and the difference between the highest paid and lowest paid jobs.

NOTE: When you use **The Method** you begin by placing each position/job in the appropriate Job Category and then follow the above procedures. You have up to six (6) grades per Category and you do not have to use them all. The number will be determined for you once you have evaluated each and come up with a numerical rating which then determines the grade.

#3: Establish a range per grade

Set a minimum and maximum range for each grade. The maximum of one grade may overlap the minimum of another and vice versa. A common spread has the minimum rate of 85% of midpoint and maximum of 115%, but it can be set at whatever the employer feels is acceptable. Many companies will average the midpoints (from salary survey data) of jobs in that grade to help establish a range for that grade. For example, a customer service position, a receptionist position and a mail clerk position may all be included in the same grade, and the averages of their midpoints from salary survey resources may be the midpoint you wish to set for that grade. Alternatively, if you are a software development company with many programmers on staff, you may have a range just for programmers and, if paying at market, may wish to use the midpoint directly from the salary survey resources for programmers as your midpoint of that grade. A range that has room for many experience levels and room for advancement will make for a balanced range.

REMEMBER how things are set up with **The Method** where you work with each Job Category. Using the LTC category, we have a mechanic helper, mechanic and diesel mechanic and three different evaluation results with the mechanic helper with 200-295 points, the mechanic with 300-395 and diesel mechanic with 400-495.

Here you have a built in career pathing program. This is where we also see the advantages of Job Categories.

WHAT IS A "STEP"? Let us use an example. When we develop a pay range we designate the minimum salary at Step 1.The salary for Step 2 is 5% more than Step 1, the midpoint salary is at Step 4 or 15% above minimum, and Step 7 is at maximum or 30% above the minimum. *You can extend the range beyond 30% as well as change the 5%.That is a decision you make when putting Base Pay in place.*

#4: Create pay grade chart

Using the sum of the minimum and the maximum, calculate the midpoint by simply dividing that sum by two ([Max + Min} / 2 = Midpoint). You now have the key elements of your grade range determined.

NOTE: With **The Method** you would have a set of grade charts for each Job Category.

#5: Review and amend

Determine how often the pay grade will be reviewed and how often adjustments will be made. Annual salary and salary structure increase projections can be used to adjust as needed. Pay grades are typically reviewed every one to three years.

This is where you can see the value of the Maintenance Program.

Pay Range Uses

Here is how steps are used:

In-hiring – The first step is set at 15% below the market or midpoint and gives an opportunity to raise workers to the midpoint in even increments over a set period of time. One recommended program is to in-hire at the minimum, then in six (6) months either terminate for failure to perform or raise to the next step. Finally, raise to the midpoint value in two (2) six (6) month intervals, so the midpoint rate is achieved in 18 months. Other variations can, of course, be worked out.

Granting merit increases – This can be done uniformly for performance either annually to the midpoint rate or the maximum or at a slower rate once the midpoint value has been reached. If an open range is used (no steps) above the midpoint value, varying amounts can be granted as merit increases. Obviously if all employees are permitted to rise to the top in time, the payroll will be inflated above the midpoint.

Promotion –Employees who are to be promoted can be fit into the higher skill level at a step rate above their current earnings without too great an increase. The usual method is to grant the worker the equivalent of one (1) step in his/her current skill level or grade plus that amount which will bring him/her to the higher of the two (2) steps between which his/her pay rate falls in the higher skill level.

The maximum – This is the stated amount above which the organization is not willing to pay to have work at any given skill level performed.

Conversion Costs

There are several options to be considered when computing the cost to convert from your present pay plan to the new Base Pay plan.

#1 Step to Step Conversion

This is the most expensive and most illogical conversion method. This says: if a worker is at any step in the existing pay plan, that worker will be assigned to the *same step* in the new Base Pay. This will result in inordinate pay increases since the new schedule is based on current market pay and has been constructed to permit both inuring below market and extra pay above market for better than average performance.

#2 Pay Matching

This method is the most equitable and is the one recommended. In this method each worker's pay is preserved to the maximum extent possible by bringing the worker to that step on the new Base Pay which is both closest and higher than his/her current pay rate. There are some exceptions:

a. If the worker is below the new minimum, he/she is paid the minimum.
b. If the worker is over the maximum, he/she is kept at current rate and "red-circled" until the Base Pay, through future surveys, is raised enough to include this worker's pay. Then the normal conversion is made as above. This also means "red-circles" employees receive only a portion of economic increases until they are incorporated into the Base Pay. Since the worker exceeds the maximum he/she is overpaid for work assigned and may be qualified for promotion.
c. If the increase to raise the worker to the minimum is excessive (over 15%, for example) a decision can be made

to grant the increase in two steps at 6 month intervals. This will hold down conversion costs.

d. If a significant number of employees are over the maximum of the new Base Pay, several options are available:

- Drop Step 1 and add a step over the maximum to create a new maximum. This may reduce the number of "red-circled" employees. It will also drop the market rate from Step 4 to Step 3. It may also increase the cost of raising employees to the new minimum

- Add a Step 8 to Base Pay to capture more of the "red-circled" workers. Normally, there should be only a handful of "red-circled" employees. A significant percent means the organization is at or above market and has a more liberal pay policy. This requires an adjustment in the construction of Base Pay. Perhaps, only one (1) step below market for in-hiring may be what the organization policy dictates.

#3 Conversion without Pay Adjustment

Another conversion option is to create Base Pay as described above and move all workers into the new structure at their current pay. They will, of course, fall in between the steps. Then, as each worker becomes eligible during the year for pay adjustment, he/she is given enough of an increase to bring him/her to the step higher than current pay. This is the least expensive and not recommended because it combines merit increases with economic adjustment. This destroys the true concept of merit increases and delays correction to prevailing market conditions.

#4 Costs

Normally, conversion costs average 3% to 5% of payroll. If the organization is substantially below market and wants to remain there, the Base Pay can be shifted so the market rate is at Step 5 or Step 6 rather than Step 4. If so, the organization can then decide to move the market rate back to Step 4 over a two (2) or three (3) period in order to reduce conversion costs. It must be remembered that:

a. The conversion cost replaces any so called "Cost of Living" increases which the organization may have been granting in the past. These will not be given again under the process herein proposed since an economic adjustment based on market pay is substituted on an annual basis.
b. The turnover rate which may be in part caused by low or non-competitive pay can be expected to drop. This saves real dollars since any one replacement of a worker costs from $200 to even thousands when all administrative and overhead costs are calculated.
c. By moving to an annual economic adjustment program plus a realistic budgeted, true merit increase program based on performance, and organization can save real dollars.

Supervisory – Managerial Pay Structure

#1 Pay Relationship

The development of a Base Pat for Supervisors and Managers should be based on the establishment of a relationship with those supervised. There are several alternatives.

a. A percent differential over those supervises and an extension of this up through all levels of management. This option has the advantage of being able to differentiate among Supervisors at the same structural level but with varying numbers and levels of workers directed. For example, not all first level Supervisors should necessarily be paid identical rates just because they are organizationally on a par.

b. Another option is to set a flat dollar rate over those directed. The weakness in the option is the difficulty in agreeing upon and maintaining this flat rate differential.

#2 Structure

The Base Pay structure has the same basic considerations as for the other Job Categories. These are:

a. An annual adjustment which can either be based upon the same economic increase given the workers supervised or can be based upon a differential (percent) over the highest level supervised. This latter method would preserve the originally established differential whereas the former method may not.

b. The creation of a salary range for Supervisors which will permit granting of merit increases for those deemed to have performed above an established standard. Normally this could either be in equal steps or an open range within which increases can be granted.

c. Establishment of both an minimum and a maximum for both control and budget purposes. This will also enable the management to maintain the differential among supervisory levels. Normally, supervisory ranges are short, i.e. 3 or 4 steps and the time intervals for merit advancement longer than for other Job Categories, i.e., two (2) years to be eligible for consideration.

Conversion

a. The same technique should be used as for other Job Categories, i.e. either to the minimum or to a point or step in the range above the current rate of pay.
b. The cost of conversion can be computed readily since the number of Supervisors is normally not large.

WE CAN DO THE WORK FOR YOU THROUGH

JOB EVALUATION MADE EASY....

…..where we write your job descriptions, evaluate them to determine internal ranking, develop a pay structure for your company and provide you on-going external market salary information. All of this for a set cost per job description and provided in individual job reports.

Want to learn more and request free sample reports?

CONTACT:

Ray Temple at raytemple@cfl.rr.com

Printed in Great
Britain
by Amazon